Problematizing the Foreign Shop: Justifications for Restricting the Migrant Spaza Sector in South Africa

Vanya Gastrow

SAMP MIGRATION POLICY SERIES NO. 80

Series Editor: Prof. Jonathan Crush

Southern African Migration Programme (SAMP)
2018

AUTHOR

Vanya Gastrow is a Postdoctoral Research Fellow in the Department of Public Law at the University of Cape Town.

ACKNOWLEDGEMENTS

The author would like to thank Mohamed Aden Osman, Dr Roni Amit, Sakhiwo 'Toto' Gxabela, Wanda Bici and Fundiswa Hoko for their support towards the research, and Prof Jonathan Crush and Bronwen Dachs for their editorial assistance.

Published by the Southern African Migration Programme, International Migration Research Centre, Balsillie School of International Affairs, Waterloo, Ontario, Canada samponline.org

First published 2018

ISBN 978-1-920596-43-9

Cover photo by Thom Pierce for the Growing Informal Cities Project

Production by Bronwen Dachs Muller, Cape Town

Printed by Print on Demand, Cape Town

CONTENTS   PAGE

EXECUTIVE SUMMARY

Small businesses owned by international migrants and refugees are often the target of xeno-phobic hostility and attack in South Africa. This has led various governance actors includ-ing the police, government ministers and provincial premiers to call for the stricter regu-lation of these enterprises. This report examines the problematization of migrant-owned businesses in South Africa, and the regulatory efforts aimed at curtailing their economic activities. In so doing, it sheds light on the complex ways in which xenophobic fears are generated and manifested in the country's social, legal and political orders.

Spaza shops are informal grocery shops that operate in most of the country's low-income neighbourhoods, and provide food and other common household items including bread, milk, canned goods and soap. This report focuses on spazas that are owned and/or operated by refugees and migrants to the country, which have been at the centre of conten-tion in South Africa over the past decade. The report is based on qualitative field research in three field sites (Kraaifontein, Khayelitsha and Philippi) in Cape Town, and in several small towns in the Western Cape province, between 2010 and 2013. The research focused on the ability of migrant shopkeepers to access justice in the Western Cape and comprised approx-imately 200 interviews with migrant traders, South African residents, police, prosecutors, legal aid attorneys and local authorities. As the large majority of migrant spaza shopkeepers in the research area were from Somalia, most migrant interviewees were Somali.

During the course of the research, it became clear that many local authorities and police officers had responded to attacks on migrant-owned spazas by attempting to curtail their business activities. This report therefore begins by tracing how formal and informal gov-ernance interventions targeting migrant spaza shopkeepers have emerged over the past decade. The earliest publicized regulatory intervention aimed at curbing these spaza shops took place in Masiphumelele in 2006 in the aftermath of xenophobic riots in the township. An informal agreement was brokered between South African and migrant spaza business owners in which the latter were permitted to operate on condition that no new migrant shops opened in the township. Similar agreements followed in townships across Cape Town (including Khayelitsha, Strand, Gugulethu, Philippi East, and Bloekombos and Wal-lacedene in Kraaifontein), and in other towns and cities in the Western Cape and Eastern Cape provinces. Although aimed at promoting peace, these interventions are problematic because they discriminate against migrant traders and fall outside legal frameworks guar-anteeing their right to trade.

At provincial and national levels, policy and regulatory efforts have intensified in recent years. In March 2013, the Department of Trade and Industry published a Licensing of Businesses Bill calling on all businesses in the country to possess licences and effectively excluding most migrants from participation in the informal economy. This controversial bill was eventually withdrawn after widespread opposition from formal business and non-governmental organizations. Then, in 2014, the department issued a National Informal Business Upliftment Strategy, which sought to address what it called the "foreign trader challenge" through measures including restricting migrants from operating small businesses. Condemnation of migrant-owned spazas has also come from an ad hoc parliamentary committee formed to investigate the causes of xenophobic violence and the Inter-Ministerial Committee on Migration. Most recently, the South African parliament enacted the Refugees Amendment Act of 2017, which prohibits asylum seekers from operating businesses in South Africa, and grants them only a very limited right to work.

The report then examines the reasons provided by national and local governance actors for their efforts to restrict migrant-owned spazas and argues that these justifications are often misleading and do not provide a coherent picture. Justifications for curbing migrant shops usually fall into four categories:

- Shops supposedly close business opportunities for South Africans and thus cause harm to local economies. However, research in the field sites indicated that many parties benefit economically from these shops, including South African landlords, wholesalers and consumers. Governance actors largely ignore these contributions and present a distorted picture of the shops' economic footprint.

- Migrants engage in illegal activities, such as breaching by-laws, not possessing business licences, possessing unregistered firearms, and unfair competition. However, many of these claims are exaggerated or unsubstantiated.

- The expansion of migrant spaza shops has led to increased rates of business robbery in the country. However, clamping down on victims of crime through regulation, as opposed to designing strategies that target offenders, is a questionable approach to addressing crime.

- Curbing migrant spaza shops through increased regulation will prevent xenophobic and other targeted attacks on these shops. Again, this entails penalizing and stigmatizing victims of crime, as opposed to rooting out the perpetrators.

In sum, the stated justifications for curbing migrant-owned spaza shops through greater regulation are often exaggerated, misleading or poorly reasoned.

Interviews in the field sites suggest that the foreign spaza shop "threat" is largely a symptom of devolved political authority and growing socio-economic discontent. While a number of residents in the field sites harboured negative attitudes towards migrant shops, the issue was not seen as of great urgency or importance. Few, if any, of the South Africans interviewed recalled ever having discussed migrant spaza shops at street committee meetings. Instead, acute hostility was felt mainly by South African spaza shopkeepers who claimed that migrant-owned shops were undermining their livelihoods. Yet, it is still relatively easy for South African spaza retailers' associations and other local political actors to incite residents to attack migrant shops. Many township residents in the field sites were frustrated with their socio-economic conditions and the shops served as a convenient target for those wishing to vent their discontent over their life circumstances. The shops represented a form of economic mobility that eluded many residents and could be attacked with impunity because of the social and political isolation of the migrant traders.

Although the selective targeting of migrant shops by local residents is xenophobic, the primary intention of most of those carrying out these attacks is to express feelings of anger, access free goods, and communicate their discontent to the country's political establishment. Anxious governance actors respond by attempting to curtail these shops through legal and extra-legal regulatory interventions. This has the effect of appeasing South African traders and preventing them from inciting further violence. It also demonstrates to township residents that the state and ruling party are "putting South African citizens first", and tacitly attributes township economic woes to foreign forces. These findings illustrate how weak state legitimacy in contexts of widespread socio-economic discontent and inequality can erode constitutional frameworks and generate hostility towards migrants and other vulnerable groups.

INTRODUCTION

> *"You cannot run away from the fact that there are underlying issues and that our people are being squeezed out by these foreign shop owners. Non-South Africans should not be allowed to buy or run spaza shops or larger businesses without having to comply with certain legislated prescripts." – Small Business Development Minister Lindiwe Zulu (2015)[1]*

Migrants from other countries operating small businesses in South Africa are often the target of popular hostility and violent crime.[2] Several studies have highlighted the existence of xenophobia towards migrants in South Africa, and antagonism towards migrant traders and spaza shops in particular.[3] This report furthers our understanding of the nature of xenophobia in South Africa by exploring how political leaders and state authorities problematize migrant-owned small businesses and attempt to curb their economic activities through regulatory interventions. In particular, it focuses on the experiences of spaza shopkeepers. Spaza shops are small informal grocery shops that operate in low-income neighbourhoods and supply residents with basic food and household items such as bread, milk, canned goods and soft drinks. By assessing perceptions of the migrant trader "threat" in South Africa, this report sheds light on the complexity of xenophobia in the country and its interplay with multiple socio-economic and political factors.

The report is based on qualitative fieldwork carried out between 2010 and 2013 in Cape Town and small towns in the Western Cape province, as well as desktop research of media reports and policy documents relating to migrant informal businesses. The fieldwork was conducted as part of a broader study on the ability of migrant traders to access formal and informal justice mechanisms in the aftermath of crime.[4] During the course of the research, it became evident that migrant-owned spaza shops were informally regulated in many of Cape Town's townships. This was largely an outcome of shops being viewed as a social and economic threat by a number of parties including South African retailers' associations, police and local government officials. This report is adapted from the larger study and sets out how governance interventions targeting migrant businesses have emerged over the past decade, the stated reasons for these strategies, and further underlying factors contributing to anxieties over migrant spaza shops in South Africa.

METHODOLOGY

Research was carried out in three field sites in Cape Town – Khayelitsha, Philippi and Kraai-fontein (Bloekombos and Wallacedene) – as well as several small towns in the Western Cape (Ceres, Caledon, Prince Alfred Hamlet, Tulbagh and Vredenberg). Approximately 200 interviews were conducted, including with 66 Somali traders, 65 South African residents, 20 police officers, prosecutors, local councillors and legal aid attorneys. South African spaza shopkeepers were not interviewed as local activists in the field sites warned that this could reignite conflict and mobilization against migrant traders. Four meetings of Somali and South African spaza shopkeepers in Khayelitsha, where the regulation of migrant spaza shops in the township was discussed, were attended in March and April 2012.

Almost all migrant spaza shopkeepers interviewed were from Somalia, as Somalis made up the large majority of migrant shopkeepers in Cape Town at the time of the research. According to an audit carried out by Philippi East police station in 2011, for example, Somalis operated 70% of migrant spaza shops in the station's jurisdiction (57 of the 82 shops).[5] The remaining shops were operated by different nationalities including Burundians (nine shops), Ethiopians (seven shops), and Bangladeshis (three shops). The Somali Association of South Africa identified some Somali traders for interview and additional respondents were interviewed via referrals. Other migrant spaza shopkeepers interviewed included two Bangladeshis, an Ethiopian, a Burundian and a Jamaican. South African and Somali research assistants helped in the interviews in the field sites and in Somali neighbourhoods in Bellville and Mitchells Plain. Interviews were conducted with various South African residents who were outside their homes or on the street when the researchers were in the neighbourhood. The aim was to obtain a range of opinions not limited to specific social networks.

GOVERNANCE INTERVENTIONS AIMED AT CURTAILING MIGRANT SMALL BUSINESSES

Since the mid-2000s, various governance actors – including political leaders, municipal officials, the police and NGOs – have attempted to curtail migrant spaza shops in South Africa through regulatory interventions. Many consider these shops to be more of a threat than an economic asset or opportunity. To understand these views, this section of the report outlines the history of formal and informal governance interventions in the country.

It illustrates the numerous, varied and at times unlawful ways in which governance actors have attempted to hinder migrants' business activities and reduce their ability to compete in the spaza market.

THE MASIPHUMELELE INTERVENTION

The earliest publicized governance intervention aimed at curtailing migrant spaza trade in South Africa took place in Masiphumelele in 2006. The intervention followed riots in the Cape Town township, which included mob attacks on migrant-owned shops and saw an estimated 70 foreign-national residents (mostly Somalis) forced to evacuate their shops and homes.[6] Against this backdrop, several parties came together to seek a way of rein-troducing migrant traders into the neighbourhood. The ensuing Masiphumelele conflict intervention process was led by the office of the Western Cape Premier and its director-ate for social dialogue and human rights. The directorate appointed a non-governmental organization, Africa Unite, to mediate between South African and Somali spaza traders in Masiphumelele.[7]

The intervention was documented in a Western Cape provincial government report, which attributed the conflict largely to the business activities of migrants, in particular their "influx" into the area, and the "unfair" competition they posed to South African spazas.[8] This situation was supposedly exacerbated by factors such as poverty in Masiphumelele, making anxieties over access to resources more intense. The report stated that the conflict in Masiphumele was not isolated, as "other communities in the Western Cape are up in arms over a perceived take-over by Somali refugees and a noticeable threat to their economic survival."[9] It chastised South African landlords for renting their properties to migrants:

> Landlords operate from a different power base as the ordinary person who is landless. Landlords also have the power to abuse this privilege, which might often lead to an attitude of oblivion with regard to the aspiration for social and economic justice.[10]

The intervention led to several workshops convened by Africa Unite in October 2006 that involved Masiphumelele community leaders as well as migrant and South African spaza shopkeepers.[11] One of the outcomes was an agreement on "future business arrange-ments in Masiphumelele."[12] Although the report does not set out the specific terms of this agreement, migrant spaza traders and media articles said that it prohibited any new migrant spaza shops from opening in the township, with the number of migrant-owned shops restricted to 15.[13]

The report further stressed that "the commitment to non-partisanship does not imply that interventions [sic] strategies should be neutral with respect to violence, the rule of law and constitutional rights."[14] However, no clear action was taken against the perpetrators of violence. In addition, trade agreements were negotiated that fell outside of the purview of the law. By-laws regulating trade in Masiphumelele do not distinguish between traders on the basis of their nationality and many migrant shopkeepers were asylum seekers and refugees who were legally entitled to work in the country.[15] The prohibition on new migrant-owned shops therefore infringed their legal right to trade and discriminated against them on the basis of their nationality. A representative of Islamic Relief Worldwide, which was tasked with providing emergency relief to migrant traders, described the agreement as "flagrantly unconstitutional."[16] As he explained:

> Unfortunately the Somalis, who wanted to move back to Masiphumelele, had no bargaining power. The failure of government to protect them from attacks basically had them agreeing to whatever was tabled… I cannot say it was a fair negotiation, but at least there is a semblance of peace.[17]

OTHER INTERVENTIONS

The Masiphumelele conflict intervention heralded a number of similar efforts across Cape Town to address hostility towards migrant spaza shopkeepers through informal prohibitions against new shops. This was particularly evident in the aftermath of the May 2008 nationwide xenophobic riots. During these riots, South African spaza shopkeepers in Strand, about 50 kilometres outside Cape Town, targeted migrant competitors in the area by sending them letters demanding that they close their businesses.[18] This caused all migrants – not only the spaza shopkeepers – to evacuate the area, with many residents looting shops while the owners fled.[19]

The violence in Masiphumelele and Strand demonstrated that frustrated South African traders had the ability to unleash broader social unrest and violence. This, in turn, placed pressure on the police, political leaders and local government officials to find ways of intervening to prevent a repetition of such attacks. The urgency was intensified by widespread murders and targeted attacks against migrant spaza shopkeepers in the city.[20]

In August 2008, when threats of xenophobia emerged in Khayelitsha, the police responded immediately. A South African retailers' association called Zanokhanyo Retailers' Association (Zanokhanyo) delivered letters to migrant spaza shopkeepers in Khayelitsha ordering them to cease trading. The letters demanded that migrant spaza shop owners close their businesses from 25 August to 14 September 2008, during which the future of their shops would be discussed.[21] When notified about the letters, the police in Khayelitsha took preventative measures and arrested several leaders of Zanokhanyo. Despite the rapid response, the police intervention in Khayelitsha had a similar outcome to that in Masiphumelele.

Those arrested were released and given suspended sentences, on condition that they enter into mediation with representatives of the Somali community. The police appointed a church minister affiliated to the police station to act as mediator.[22] The outcome was that migrant and South African retailers came to an agreement that no new spaza shops could open in Khayelitsha without the approval of Zanokhanyo and a "Somali committee."[23] The Masiphumelele and Khayelitsha interventions were mirrored in many other townships across Cape Town. In August 2009, threatening letters were sent to migrant spaza shopkeepers in Gugulethu. In response, the office of the United Nations High Commissioner for Refugees (UNHCR) and a non-government organization called the Anti-Eviction Campaign mediated an agreement between South African and Somali shopkeepers in the neighbourhood. This agreement prohibited new migrant spaza shops from opening in the area and stipulated that existing traders fix their prices to those of their South African competitors. The agreement also provided that migrant-owned shops could only comprise 30% of the spaza shop market in Gugulethu, and that their businesses needed to be located at least 100 metres from South African shops.[24]

This agreement appeared to be a clear breach of South Africa's competition laws, which forbid price fixing and market division (i.e. the dividing up of markets by business competitors through allocating territories or specific types of services).[25] However, the Competition Commission's response to the agreement was muted, with a spokesperson telling the Cape Times newspaper that not all agreements restricting competition violated competition laws. She said that the commission could initiate an investigation if there was "reason to believe the law is being breached."[26] However, no investigation was ever launched.[27]

In 2011, agreements prohibiting new migrant-owned shops were entered into in both Kraaifontein and Philippi.[28] The Kraaifontein agreement barred new shops from opening in the townships of Bloekombos and Wallacedene, and was established following a meeting called by the South African National Civic Organization (SANCO) at a local police station. In Philippi, South African traders delivered letters to South African landlords under the banner of SANCO informing them to instruct their foreign-national tenants to cease trading by 30 June 2011.[29] After the deadline had passed, South African traders proceeded to forcibly close down migrant businesses, but were stopped by police.[30] Thereafter, representatives of migrant and South African retailers met at Philippi East police station and agreed that migrant traders could stay in the area as long as they did not open any new shops. The retailers as well as the police would monitor this measure.[31]

The agreements entered into in many of Cape Town's neighbourhoods, including Masiphumelele, Khayelitsha, Strand, Gugulethu, Kraaifontein and Philippi, tended to follow the same formula. South African traders threatened havoc and police responded by hastily setting up mediations. Mediators included NGOs, religious leaders and the UNHCR, and the meetings were usually attended by a host of other parties including municipal law enforcement officers, SANCO, the national Department of Economic Development, and the city's Disaster Risk Management Centre. Most agreements related specifically to Somali spaza shops. However, the Khayelitsha agreement included Ethiopian shops (although Ethiopians' representatives rarely, if ever, attended meetings), and there was unresolved debate in Philippi about whether Burundian shops were covered by the agreement.

Local agreements restricting trade by migrant shopkeepers also existed further afield. Somali shopkeepers in the Saldanha Bay Municipality on the West Coast, for example, said that similar rules governed the spaza market in the region.[32] According to media reports, agreements prohibiting new migrant spaza shops were negotiated in Mbekweni in Paarl (in 2009), and in Port Elizabeth (in 2011) and Bisho (in 2012) in the Eastern Cape province.[33] The Bisho agreement had the backing of the then provincial MEC for local government, Mlibo Qoboshiyane, who described it as justified and said that it should be enforced.[34]

At the same time as local agreements were being entered into across the Western Cape and Eastern Cape provinces, migrant spaza shops gained increased political attention at provincial and national levels.[35] Like their local counterparts, provincial and national government officials perceived these shops as a threat that needed to be curtailed. Minister of Police Bheki Cele said at an October 2011 meeting of police officers in Khayelitsha that "our people have been economically displaced; all these spaza shops are not run by locals." He added that, "one day, our people will revolt, and we've appealed to DTI [Department of Trade and Industry] to do something about it."[36]

In June 2012, the African National Congress in the Western Cape called on the state to cut the number of migrant-owned spaza shops in the province's townships, noting that its local branches felt that South African potential shop owners were "losing out."[37] These demands bore fruit in March 2013, when the Department of Trade and Industry (DTI) published a draft Licensing of Businesses Bill. The bill provided that all businesses in the country (formal and informal) should possess a government-issued licence and was widely perceived as aimed at curtailing migrant-owned spaza shops in the informal sector.[38] It gave local authorities wide discretion to issue licences, as well as the power to revoke traders' business licences permanently in the event that shops were threatened by public violence. However, after much outcry from South Africa's business community and NGOs, the bill was never promulgated.

Later in 2013 the DTI circulated a draft National Informal Business Upliftment Strategy (Nibus), which among other things sought to address the "foreign trader challenge."[39] A suggested response included following the example of Ghana where foreigners are for the most part barred from operating small businesses.[40] To implement Nibus, the State President in 2014 created the Department of Small Business Development and its minister – Lindiwe Zulu – immediately called for the increased regulation of migrant businesses.[41] Further high-level support for the curtailment of migrant businesses was given by the Premier of North West province, Supra Mahumapelo, who in March 2016 declared that all migrant spaza businesses in the province should be confiscated and transferred to South Africans.[42] These hostile local, regional and national level sentiments towards migrant businesses were finally given formal legislative backing in December 2017, when Parliament enacted the Refugees Amendment Act. The Act prohibits asylum seekers from opening businesses in the country, essentially barring large numbers of migrants from being able to open shops. It remains to be seen how the state will go about implementing these restrictive provisions designed to make South Africa a less attractive safe haven for refugees.

The informal and formal attempts by governance actors at all levels to regulate migrant-owned spaza shops are a reflection of anxiety among state officials and political leaders about the economic activities of international migrants and refugees. They view the shops as a threat that requires quick and radical action and, as a result, they have either supported or condoned extra-legal and unconstitutional attempts to restrict migrants' small businesses. The next section of the report investigates what motivates these actions through exploring their stated justification for greater regulation of migrant-owned spaza shops.

JUSTIFICATIONS FOR CURBING MIGRANT SPAZAS

Local officials and political leaders engaged in the governance of the spaza sector have provided many reasons for the supposed threat to the country's interests posed by migrant-owned spaza shops. These can be grouped into four general arguments: (a) the shops cause economic harm to South Africans; (b) the migrant shopkeepers engage in illegal activities; (c) the shops are responsible for increased rates of business robbery in the country; and (d) their presence provokes South Africans into acts of violence and looting.

ECONOMIC HARM

Many governance actors have said that migrant spaza shops are harmful to local economies and inhibit job creation. They reference widespread complaints by South African spaza shopkeepers who say they are unable to compete. Accordingly, many policy makers complain that migrant shopkeepers restrict economic opportunities for aspirant South African shopkeepers in the market.[43] This is heightened by claims that migrants enjoy significant competitive advantages over South African retailers, such as having more expansive business networks.[44] Other alleged economic harm caused by migrant shopkeepers include that they send remittances to their home countries rather than spending their total income in South Africa, and do not contribute taxes to government coffers.

Over the past decade, many South African spaza shops have certainly experienced losses in income and/or closed down. The increase in foreign-national competition may have played a role in this, along with rising food prices and the growth in the number of supermarkets in township neighbourhoods. However, South African retailer representatives in Gugulethu asserted that Somali shopkeepers were the cause of many shop closures:

> Somali traders sell their goods far cheaper than the local traders. [South African spaza retailers] also claim that Somalis would pitch their shops closer to the shops of the locals and as their wares are sold cheaper, buyers turn to buy from the Somali shopkeepers rather than from the locals. In this manner, local shopkeepers are forced to close their shops because they are unable to compete with the Somalis.[45]

Many South African residents interviewed in this study believe that migrant spaza shops have restricted opportunities for South Africans by saturating the spaza market. They maintain that this lessened South Africans' chances of initiating small grocery businesses to their economic detriment. Many migrant spaza traders send portions of their income to relatives in their home countries, rather than spending it all in South Africa. It is also feasible that migrant spaza traders (like their South African competitors) do not pay income tax. However, many traders' incomes fall below the income tax threshold of ZAR75,000 per year, which means that they are not obliged to pay income tax in the first place.

These arguments about the economic harm of migrant spaza operations are highly selective, ignoring the fact that they provide many benefits to local communities and economies. For example, these shopkeepers have enabled South African township residents to become landlords. None of the spaza traders interviewed for this study owned the properties from which they traded. Instead they leased their premises from South Africans, many of whom had previously been spaza shopkeepers. The landlords interviewed said that these shops benefitted them as foreign traders paid significant rent and they could earn passive income without having to work. This particularly advantaged those who struggled to hold down wage-earning jobs, such as pensioners, single mothers and community volunteers.

Migrant spaza shops presented other local economic advantages. South African residents described how they offered lower prices and better services than their local counterparts. Service advantages included offering credit, giving exact change, having shorter queues, selling goods in flexible quantities (for example, one tea bag or an egg as opposed to a box), offering hampers (collections of goods sold at a discount), possessing broader product ranges, and being less likely to run out of stock.

South African suppliers, manufacturers, wholesalers and employees also benefit from migrant spaza shops. For example, the manager of the wholesaler Philippi Cash and Carry said that the business employed 103 South Africans and only two foreign nationals - himself (an Israeli) and a Somali translator.[46] He said that the expansion of migrant-owned spaza shops in Cape Town had improved his sales and enabled him to hire more South African staff. However, governance actors rarely consider the economic advantages of migrant shops in their proclamations.

In November 2015, for example, the Inter-Ministerial Committee on Migration informed the parliamentary ad hoc committee probing violence against migrants that "foreign nationals were dominating trade in certain sectors such as consumable goods in informal settlements which has had a negative impact on unemployed and low skilled South

Africans."[47] It made no mention of any economic contributions by migrant traders to local economies.

It is not difficult to understand why South African spaza shopkeepers are alarmed by the expansion of migrant shops and mobilize against them. Competition is an unpleasant encounter for many businesses, especially those struggling to stay afloat. What is surprising is that these frustrations have taken overwhelming precedence over the interests of other parties, such as landlords, wholesalers and consumers. Given the complexity of the local economic context and the varied parties involved, it is not clear why governance actors have given such primacy to the interests of South African spaza shopkeepers. This suggests that concerns other than economics have played a role in motivating intervention.

ILLEGAL ACTIVITY

Another stated motivation provided by governance actors for curbing migrant spaza shops is that the traders engage in illegal activities. Police officials, local authorities and political leaders often argue that migrant spaza traders do not pay taxes, are illegal immigrants, do not adhere to by-laws and health and safety regulations, lack valid permits and licences, possess firearms unlawfully, import goods illegally, trade in counterfeit and illicit goods, and generally engage in "unfair" trading practices. For instance, the Ad Hoc Joint Committee on Probing Violence against Foreign Nationals asserted that migrant traders succeed in part because they undermine competition through "forming monopolies, evading taxes, avoiding customs and selling illegal and expired goods."[48] The committee accordingly called for improved policing of counterfeit goods and container shops, and tighter monitoring of business permits and by-laws.[49]

Several senior politicians have similarly depicted migrant shopkeepers as legally delinquent. For example, Minister of Trade and Industry Rob Davies accused foreign-national businesses of selling "goods that are imported, probably illegally ... are not made in South Africa, that are not proudly South African."[50] Likewise, Gauteng Premier David Makhura argued in his 2018 State of the Province Address that:

> Another major problem facing township businesses is the mushrooming of unregulated businesses owned by foreign nationals. This is a matter we must address boldly and decisively to enforce by-laws and trading regulations. Many township entrepreneurs are being squeezed out of businesses by these unlawfully operating foreigner-owned businesses.[51]

Former President Jacob Zuma said that migrant businesses in Gauteng provoked South Africans to attack them in early 2015 through their unlawful behaviour:

> *Nobody was saying 'we don't want you in these shops'. Only when this incident [i.e. the shooting of a 14-year-old alleged robber by a Somali shopkeeper with an unregistered firearm] happens, then it triggered that problem. ... We need to help the foreigners. One - so that they must understand that they couldn't provoke. Two - they themselves should have things within the law.*[52]

Not all migrant spaza shop owners comply with the law. Police in the field sites claimed that many possess unregistered firearms, for example. Some foreign-national shopkeepers said they kept firearms on their premises for self-defence. This is largely in response to violent crime, coupled with the fact that migrant traders generally lack access to registered firearms, which are the preserve of South African citizens and permanent residents.[53] In addition, many spaza shops trade in illicit cigarettes, which South African tobacco manufacturers release onto the market without disclosure to the revenue service.[54]

However, portrayals of migrant spaza shop owners as failing to comply with laws are commonly erroneous or exaggerated. Counterfeit trading is seen more among informal street traders and small businesses dealing in clothing and electronics, than in the spaza grocery shop sector. In this sector, shops tend to sell food and household items such as sugar, bread, oil, flour and maize meal, which are manufactured in South Africa and purchased from formal wholesalers. Also, many migrant shopkeepers are asylum seekers or refugees with permits, and are entitled to work in the country. For example, in Cape Town the majority of migrant spaza shopkeepers are Somalis who, according to the UNHCR, had a refugee recognition rate averaging 84% between 2001 and 2013.[55]

Another common claim is that migrant spaza shops engage in unfair business practices. However, those in the fieldwork sites rely on conventional business practices such as price competition, forming partnerships and accommodating customer needs, which are hardly "unfair" or monopolistic. They also commonly comply with township by-laws. This is because many township zoning schemes permit the establishment of businesses on residential properties on condition that the dominant use of the property remains residential and the business does not disturb neighbours or interfere with the amenity of the neighbourhood.

In addition, many spaza shops are not required to possess permits or licences. In Cape Town, only businesses operating from demarcated trading bays in public spaces such as markets, train stations and pavements need permits from the city.[56] Business licences in the city are only required for traders who sell prepared meals, prepared food on site (such as delis, takeout stands and restaurants), or offer health and entertainment services (such as massage parlours). The city's environmental health office said that spaza shops did not need business licences because they sold pre-packed foods.[57]

Responding to concerns over violence against migrant traders in 2015, the Minister of Small Business Development, Lindiwe Zulu, claimed that the attacks diverted public attention from the valid frustrations of South African business owners that migrants did not trade according to the law.[58] However, in an interview she could not clearly explain which laws were being breached, stating, "that's why I'm saying we need to fast track that, because the regulations are falling short in terms of ensuring that there's proper re-zoning, there's proper infrastructure."[59]

The South African Police Service (SAPS) is cognizant that migrant spaza shop owners generally comply with by-laws. In its input to the National Informal Business Upliftment Strategy (Nibus), it acknowledged that shops located on private properties do not contravene street trading by-laws:

> Some of these informal businesses [i.e. businesses which are not regulated in terms of the Business Act or White Paper] are operated on private premises and thus cannot be charged in terms of contravention of the by-law on Street Trading, as it does not apply to private premises and this makes it difficult to implement and ensure strict compliance by SAPS (parenthesis in the original).[60]

Many SAPS officials and law enforcement officers interviewed in Cape Town stressed that township spaza shops did not need business licences or permits to operate. The station commander of Khayelitsha police station, for example, said that the township was a "free trade area" and that shops did not require any official permission to open. In 2012, at a meeting between Somali and South African spaza traders in Khayelitsha, an official from the city's municipal law enforcement department noted that:

> Khayelitsha is not regulated and no trading plan has been submitted for the area. In the absence of a trading area, the area is deemed a free trading area. Because it's a free trade area we cannot tell people not to trade.[61]

He explained that government could not easily interfere with businesses being operated on private properties in townships:

> *All former disadvantaged areas, i.e. black areas, are exempted from the Land Use Planning Ordinance. Therefore no re-zoning is needed for business. So any business can run from a property, RDP or container, and people do not need to apply for re-zoning.... I want to stress: we should start pointing fingers at ourselves. They are not setting up shop on city land, but in your yards.*[62]

If some migrant spaza shopkeepers do contravene regulations by not paying taxes, or trading without a licence, it would be difficult to argue that South African spaza shopkeepers behave any differently. On the contrary, evidence suggests that South African spaza shopkeepers are less legally compliant than their migrant counterparts. For instance, at a meeting between Somali and South African shopkeepers in Khayelitsha in 2012, the meeting chairperson lamented that "there is a by-law. You need permits issued by local government. Unfortunately local people are not tending to permits, only Somalis."[63] The chairperson's remark was not completely accurate, as there is no by-law requiring spaza shops to possess permits in Cape Town, which means that many Somali traders had paid for and been issued with unnecessary trading permits. Some Somalis claimed that the Fezeka municipal office in Gugulethu had issued them with informal trading permits for a monthly fee of ZAR150. One Somali community representative said that he had assisted over 100 traders in applying for permits at the municipal office.

A survey carried out in Motherwell township in Port Elizabeth involving 64 Somali and 65 South African spaza shopkeepers found that South African spaza shops had a lower tax registration rate than migrant businesses.[64] In South Africa, all businesses are obliged to register with the revenue service within 60 days of commencing operations irrespective of whether or not they earn below the tax threshold.[65] While the study found that 74% of Somali shopkeepers were registered for income tax, only 17% of South African shopkeepers were similarly registered.[66] Also, many South African spaza shops engage in anti-competitive business practices. These include threatening their competitors with acts of violence, demanding the closure of competitors' businesses and, in extreme instances, ordering the murder of their competitors.[67] Yet governance actors voice little concern over these unfair business practices. For example, the Competition Commission failed to investigate the 2009 price-fixing agreement in Gugulethu, but did initiate a market inquiry into the economic activities of migrant retailers in 2016.[68]

Some provincial governments have tried to inhibit migrant businesses by impeding their ability to obtain business licences. For instance, migrant spaza traders in Limpopo province were prevented from acquiring business licences in 2012, as staff at local municipal offices informed them that foreign nationals did not qualify.[69] A range of state actors defended the matter in court, including the minister of police, the minister of home affairs, the national police commissioner and the standing committee for refugee affairs.[70] However, in 2014, the Supreme Court of Appeal found that the closure of the businesses was unlawful and that asylum seekers and refugees were entitled to apply for licences.

There are many instances of police breaking the law in their attempts to limit migrant spaza shops. Between November 2011 and February 2013, police fined numerous foreign-national shops in Cape Town in terms of non-existent legislation.[71] In some instances, traders were not only fined, but also arrested and detained in police holding cells for several hours. The fines, which ranged from ZAR1,000 to ZAR2,000, were penalties for trading without a licence. However, as mentioned above, spaza shops in Cape Town do not require business licences to operate. Also, senior police leaders have supported discriminatory regulatory arrangements that have no legal basis. For example, at meetings in Khayelitsha, the informal trade agreement barring new migrant-owned spaza shops was supported by the minister of police, the provincial commissioner of police and the special advisor to the minister of police.

These examples suggest that governance actors are not greatly invested in legal compliance and conformity, and that complaints over the illegality of migrant spaza shops are disingenuous. Claims of unlawful behaviour are frequently inaccurate or exaggerated, and state officials have taken active steps to inhibit the ability of shopkeepers to comply with the law. Regulatory attempts have frequently involved authorities breaching the law themselves and, at the same time, governance actors have shown little interest in the legality of South African shops.

INCREASED CRIME

A third official reason given for clamping down on migrant-owned spaza shops is that they are responsible for a dramatic increase in business robbery. A SAPS national analysis of 4,128 business robbery cases reported between September and November 2015 found that spaza or tuck shops were the businesses most frequently targeted by robbers, making up 23% of reported cases.[72] Other businesses targeted included supermarkets (12%), general dealers

(7%) and taverns, bars and shebeens (7%). Foreign nationals whose nationality could be established – mainly Ethiopians, Somalis, Bangladeshis and Pakistanis – made up 48% of business robbery victims in the country.[73] Some provinces reported higher rates of migrants affected by business robberies. For example, in the North West province, 78% of business robbery victims were foreign nationals. Robberies have also been on the increase. Official crime statistics indicate that business robberies in the Western Cape province rose from 634 cases in 2007/2008 to 1,889 cases in 2016/2017.[74] Nationally, business robberies increased from 4,384 cases in 2005/2006 to 9,836 cases in 2007/2008 to 20,680 in 2014/2015.[75]

Police have claimed that the increase in business robberies is largely attributable to the expansion of migrant spaza shops in the country. Former Western Cape Police Commissioner Arno Lamoer reported in February 2013 that:

> The proliferation of 'Spaza' shops linked to the influx of foreign nationals, particularly in townships throughout the Province, has resulted in an upsurge in business robberies and attacks on owners of the 'Spaza' shops.[76]

Criminals single out migrant spaza shops for several reasons. Firstly, migrant spaza businesses are profitable targets as they are cash enterprises that trade in fast-moving consumer goods. Other informal businesses (such as hair salons, shoe repair shops and fruit and vegetable stalls) do not possess the same quantities of cash and easily tradable products.

Second, migrant shopkeepers are vulnerable due to their social and political isolation. South African community organizations play a key role in investigating crime, adjudicating incidents, and punishing alleged culprits in townships. These structures are usually organized in the form of street committees, which are small residents' groups falling under the auspices of the South African National Civic Organization (SANCO). Their role in combatting crime is particularly important given many township residents' lack of trust in the formal justice system.

Street committee activities vary from neighbourhood to neighbourhood. Some committees work closely with the police, while others deal with crime on their own. In the shack settlement of Thabo Mbeki in Philippi East, for example, residents reported that the police played almost no role in addressing crime. Instead, a neighbourhood committee of 13 individuals organized street patrols, investigated criminal cases and called informal hearings. Punishments included banishment, beatings and, in severe cases, death. In contrast, in the nearby informal settlement of Phola Park, residents described how street committees barely functioned and police avoided the area due to the vast quantity of illegal weapons circulating in the area. As a result, suspected criminals often faced spontaneous mob beatings without being afforded a formal or informal hearing. In other areas, street committees did not play a role in adjudication or punishment, but cooperated with police in investigating crime.

When migrant spaza shopkeepers fall victim to crime, street committees offer little assistance beyond their condolences. Some residents stated that street committees failed to respond because crimes affecting migrants' shops were not seen as community concerns. The vast majority of migrant spaza shopkeepers' families live outside township neighbourhoods and their children attend different schools. Also, many shopkeepers are Muslim and therefore do not attend the same places of worship as South African township residents or socialize at the same eating or drinking venues. Residents said that migrant shopkeepers were tenants who did not stay in neighbourhoods for long and they therefore did not view them as fully rooted and invested in the community. Only three of the 71 shopkeepers interviewed had ever participated in street committee meetings. Reasons given for this included safety concerns, feeling unwelcome, and clashes with their working hours. Many township residents therefore feel detached from the experiences of migrant shopkeepers. One Khayelitsha resident said that "we don't help them because they don't help us. We are not really concerned about their problems because they are very separate from us. If someone were to kill them, we would never even know."[77] A group of youth in Philippi East said that robbing migrant spaza shops was easy.[78] They could rob the same shop repeatedly even if shopkeepers recognized them. They could not do the same with South African shops because the shopkeepers would be likely to know local community leaders who would intervene.

Police have responded to high levels of crime affecting migrant shops by clamping down on these businesses. In August 2012, police in Maropong in the North West province fined and confiscated the goods of approximately 100 migrant spaza shopkeepers.[79] A police officer said the motivation for the raids was to reduce crime statistics:

> If a R100 is stolen from a spaza shop it becomes part of house breaking statistics in the province. Illegal taverns also contribute to high crime statistics and alcohol related crime, it is for this reason that several operations throughout the province have seen many foreign nationals who operate business illegally arrested.[80]

The degree to which shops are legally compliant is unlikely to influence their suscep-tibility to robbery. This indicates that the purpose of the police interventions was not to protect the shops from being robbed through ensuring greater legal compliance, but rather to shut noncompliant businesses and thereby reduce the number of shops being robbed.

This is an extremely problematic way of addressing crime, as it targets the victims rather than the perpetrators. We might expect that the police would focus their attention on find-ing and punishing the culprits. Yet, analysis of justice system responses to crimes affecting migrant shopkeepers in Cape Town in 2010 and 2011 shows that police made very little progress in any of the victims' cases. Victims said that police would do little beyond open-ing a case. Occasionally they made arrests, but in all instances the suspects were released and the matter closed. None of the business robbery victims interviewed for this study reported successful prosecutions. Police described a number of difficulties in investigating these crimes, including language barriers and the relocation of shopkeepers, but had no clear strategies to deal with these challenges. Instead, their efforts seemed focused on curb-ing migrant spaza businesses. The preoccupation with reducing shop numbers, rather than protecting shops and targeting offenders, suggests that there are additional factors behind police calls for the increased regulation of migrant spaza shops.

REDUCING VIOLENCE

A fourth official reason for the stricter regulation of migrant spaza shops is that their pres-ence provokes South Africans into violence. On many occasions South African spaza trad-ers have threatened to wreak havoc unless migrant shops in their neighbourhoods close down. The 2009 Gugulethu agreement, for example, states that South African spaza trad-ers sent out leaflets in Gugulethu demanding that Somali traders close shop "or else they will face unpleasant consequences."[81] Meetings were subsequently organized to "warn the Gugulethu public against any action that could incite one section of the population against another."[82] The agreement further states that when Somali traders tried to pull out of nego-tiations, the UNHCR requested "another meeting, to enable it to have a discussion with the Somalis and to explain to them the need to co-operate with the local traders in order to avert any ugly situation from happening."[83] A 2012 communiqué signed by the Zanokhanyo retailers' association and the Somali retailers' association in Khayelitsha notes that infor-mal trade agreements were established in several townships in Cape Town to "bring peace, mutual co-existence and cohesion following the unfortunate and tragic events of 2008."[84] It cautions that lack of enforcement of the agreement "will breed anarchy in our community."

The potential for violence is not only cited in documentation relating to informal trade agreements, but was articulated at community meetings in Khayelitsha. At a meeting in March 2012, the chairperson noted:

> We need to work this out before it gets ugly. I just heard that there are problems in Plettenberg Bay and that there is xenophobia happening there. We do not want that in Khayelitsha and our townships.[85]

The SAPS has argued that barring migrant businesses from operating in certain areas is necessary to avert violence. Its input to Nibus, for example, states that "to reduce xenophobia associated with foreign national traders, there is a need for the strategy to influence the type of businesses that foreign nationals should run and the demarcated areas where these businesses should be active."[86] However, such a response penalizes potential victims of xenophobic violence rather than punishing those threatening or carrying out attacks. Police responses to xenophobic mob outbreaks are generally very weak. Many migrant spaza traders in the fieldwork sites said that police who arrive on the scene of looting refuse to protect their property and are only prepared to evacuate them, resulting in the destruction of their businesses. When looters are arrested, police release them without any further action. Traders said that in some instances of looting, police stood idly by or even helped themselves to goods.

Police responses to threats and attacks by South African shopkeepers are subdued. South African retailers' associations often send threatening leaflets to Somali shopkeepers or their landlords telling them to close their businesses. Instead of investigating South African retailers for sending out threatening letters, police convene mediation meetings where migrant shopkeepers are pressured into limiting their businesses. In cases where migrant spaza owners or their employees are murdered, local police stations do not have a clear strategy to deal with these crimes. One (Kraaifontein) police station did prioritize investigations into the numerous murders of migrant traders in 2010. A police investigator was assigned to all cases relating to spaza shops and gathered crime intelligence. His work led to the arrests of four South African spaza shopkeepers and seven youths who were linked to 33 criminal cases affecting migrant spaza shops.[87] The suspects were detained for several months, but were released when the state's case collapsed after one of its key witnesses (one of the youths) refused to testify in court. Errors were also identified in the ballistics evidence.[88] The police investigator believed that although the investigation had not led to any convictions, the arrests helped to prevent further attacks:

> *Somalis are no longer as afraid of South African shopkeepers because police are harsher than before and the police approach is different… If something starts like that we want it to stop. We will go right to the people we arrested before and detain them again. They got such a fright after this.*[89]

Somali shopkeepers agreed that orchestrated murders ceased after the police actions in 2010.[90] Although they entered into an informal agreement prohibiting new migrant shops the following year, the detective believed that this was a result of political pressure by SANCO and South African traders, who realized after the arrests that they could not utilize violence to drive out competition.[91]

In contrast, Khayelitsha experienced very few incidents of orchestrated attacks on Somali traders. None of the 15 Somali traders interviewed there reported incidents such as assassination-style killings or arson attacks. While police believed that there could be ulterior motives behind some business robberies, they were not in possession of any evidence.[92] Members of the Somali Retailers' Association believed that orchestrated attacks were rare in Khayelitsha. The only incident known to them was the fatal shooting of three Somali shopkeepers shortly after a hostile meeting between Somali and South African traders in October 2010.[93] Somali traders in Khayelitsha believed that they were less vulnerable to orchestrated crime because they enjoyed a greater degree of community support than in Philippi and Kraaifontein. One said that "Khayelitsha is the only area where at least we have a friendship with the black people. At least it's somewhere I can go any time… In Khayelitsha I can drive any time I want, even if it's midnight because I know the people."[94] Somalis have been in the area from as early as the mid-1990s, well before South African traders and residents perceived them as a threat. This has enabled them to form positive relationships with local residents. Also, in the aftermath of the 2008 xenophobic riots, Somali traders organized a community outreach programme, which strengthened their ties with community members and leaders.

While the prohibition of new migrant spaza shops in many townships may have placated frustrated South African traders, governance actors could have tried other strategies before selecting one that was discriminatory and undermined the rule of law. Police rarely investigated South African retailers for threatening migrant businesses, or made significant efforts to charge and prosecute looters. The efforts in Kraaifontein to prioritize investigations into the orchestrated murders of migrant retailers were not taken up in other areas.

BROADER FACTORS CONTRIBUTING TO POLITICAL ANXIETY OVER MIGRANT SPAZAS

The foregoing discussion shows that the stated justifications for curtailing migrant spaza shops are often inaccurate, contradictory or incomplete. Understanding the motives driving efforts to curb migrant spaza shops thus requires going beyond studying official reasoning to examining surrounding social and political contexts. Both Fanon and Mamdani believe that hostilities towards migrant traders in newly independent African countries during the 20th century were a symptom of broader political conditions. In particular, they argue that they were fed by postcolonial vesting of rights and entitlements in notions of indigeneity.[95] This eventually led to whole societies turning against perceived immigrants, including those from other African countries.

South Africa reflects features of Fanon and Mamdani's assertions. Notions of rights and justice in post-apartheid South Africa are often linked to claims for indigenous ownership and restitution. For example, at a rally in Cape Town on 9 February 2016, former President Jacob Zuma said:

> We need to change the economy of this country radically. We the blacks who are a majority, but we're they [sic] have very little to do with the economy. And that is the task of the ANC.[96]

Similarly, the Minister of Small Business Development, Lindiwe Zulu, has highlighted the need for back South Africans to attain economic justice. In her 2015 department budget speech, she states that:

> Twenty years since our freedom, the participation of black people in the country's economy still leaves much to be desired. Radical economic transformation is about turning this ugly picture on its head… South Africa, should, in its ownership, management and skills, reflect the active and meaningful participation of Africans in particular, and black people in general.[97]

The economic upliftment of black South Africans is a legitimate and important goal, but calls for transformation can heighten animosity towards non-nationals competing against black-owned businesses in low-income areas. Many South African spaza traders view migrant shopkeepers as undermining black economic liberation. At a meeting in Khayelitsha in 2012, for example, a South African trader complained that the municipal law enforcement department's representative was "trying to oppress the black people in this province as much as he can… it is not true that we have xenophobia, we just want to benefit from the fruits of our revolution."[98] Another South African spaza shopkeeper likened the arrival of Somali spaza shopkeepers to colonial settlers: "They [Somalis] come here rich, they find us poor and take advantage of us. It's the same as when Jan van Riebeeck came here – it's exploitation."[99]

Yet, the linking of rights to indigeneity does not adequately explain hostilities towards migrant spaza shopkeepers in South Africa. Fanon and Mamdani's analyses of postcolonial Africa depict whole populations as violently antagonistic towards foreign traders. However, acute hostilities towards migrant shopkeepers in the field sites were not widespread among residents. Instead, intense anger was mainly harboured by South African traders. Most residents, including those with negative views about foreign traders, did not feel strongly about the presence of migrant spaza shops. Many residents recognized that migrant shops' low prices and efficient services were beneficial to them. Some even offered considerable praise of these businesses. A Philippi East resident, for example, said that "Somali traders will still sell if I'm 10 cents short, but not Xhosas. This is why I like Somali shops. When they came they didn't take anyone's shop. They never actively closed down anyone's shop."[100] Up the road, another resident noted that "if it were up to me I'd make bigger facilities for foreigners to thrive because as business people they create avenues for growth and the community benefits a lot."[101] Similarly, a Kraaifontein resident argued that "foreign spaza shopkeepers have nothing but respect for residents. They keep their premises very clean, take out dirt bins and clean the street. They give a lot of credit because they know what struggling is about."[102]

At the same time, some residents do have concerns about migrant spaza shops. The most widespread grievance related to issues of personal and shop hygiene, with some residents believing that migrant traders have low levels of personal hygiene and that the bread they sell has an odd smell. Another common worry was that the expansion of migrant spaza shops had closed down avenues of economic opportunity for local residents. A resident in Lower Crossroads, Philippi East, argued that "locals cannot have self-initiated businesses because foreigners took over the market."[103] In Better Life, Philippi East, a resident said: "I have no problem with Somalis, but they should not have twenty shops in Better Life alone because it cancels the chances of local South Africans."[104]

Some residents said that migrant spaza shops offered advantages and disadvantages. A Khayelitsha resident said that they benefitted her community because of their long operating hours and low prices. At the same time, she believed that "they take away opportunities."[105] A few residents felt intense anger towards migrant spaza traders. For instance, a resident in Gugulethu compared traders to snakes, and a Philippi East resident accused them of being stingy and not supporting the community.[106] Yet, these grievances were mostly not of great importance to residents. None of the residents interviewed could recall having discussed the issue of migrant spaza shops at street committee meetings. They were largely in agreement that the primary actors mobilizing against migrant spaza shops were local South African spaza retailers.

LOCAL POLITICAL DYNAMICS BEHIND MIGRANT SPAZA REGULATION

The urgency for government, police and others to act is therefore not directly fed by local populations, but rather by a particular group with a vested stake in the spaza market. Analyzing efforts to curb migrant spaza shops thus necessitates examining local political dynamics and, in particular, the role of public violence. In order to carry out violent attacks on migrant shops, South African spaza shopkeepers often incite surrounding residents, as occurred in Masiphumelele in 2006 and in Strand in 2008. On other occasions, local political leaders orchestrate mob attacks. For instance, in February 2015, Ses'kona People's Rights Movement members looted migrant shops in Philippi East. The movement's leader defended the members' actions on the basis that a Somali national had bumped a Ses'kona protester with his car in Bellville earlier that day.[107] However, a Khayelitsha community activist noted that Ses'kona had planned the lootings in advance, with leaders instructing members to bring bags with them to protests: "People were told that go and have your bags there, we're going to loot."[108] On other occasions, residents attacked migrant spaza businesses spontaneously during strikes and service delivery protests as a means of lashing out and highlighting their discontent.[109]

Such attacks indicate popular xenophobic disregard of the rights and interests of migrant traders, but they are not necessarily an indication of widespread intense antagonism. While it is clearly apparent in their choice of targets that mob attacks are xenophobic, the immediate motivations of participants in such violence are more complex. Participation in mob violence is not necessarily motivated by direct animosity towards foreigners. Instead, crowds attack shops as a means of venting anger at government over poor social conditions, or simply to take advantage of the opportunity of accessing free goods:

> *In an informal settlement you find people who are very frustrated because of the conditions we live in, no space, no electricity, no water. Most people living in an informal settlement have an anger issue. They're always frustrated. And then you find lots of people are sitting there doing nothing. So now you come there and say let's go to that shop. Or just one person starts to throw stones. It just takes one person, most of the time they do not plan.[110]*

> *When there is something untoward happening in a typical township it catches the attention of the community, like paraffin being poured on a flame. The rest of the community will not be aware of what is happening and they will not necessarily be interested in getting to know what is happening. They will want to bring a tire to burn as well.[111]*

Violent outbursts by local residents communicate socio-economic discontent and anger to political leaders. Levels of poverty and unemployment in South Africa are high. The country has an unemployment rate of over 25%, and more than 20% of South Africans fall below the food poverty line.[112] South Africa is also one of the most economically unequal countries in the world.[113]

Migrant spazas represent a form of economic mobility and prosperity that continues to elude most ordinary township residents. By attacking these shops, residents demonstrate to political leaders their desperate economic need and the fact that non-citizens are making greater economic advances. A Khayelitsha resident said that "people are angry with the government and by committing xenophobia they think that maybe government will pay attention and meet their needs."[114] Mob violence against migrant businesses in South Africa's townships can thus be seen as a means of communicating discontent to political leaders and urging them to address township residents' economic plight. This is heightened by the fact that political promises to address the economic legacies of apartheid have largely been unmet. Residents' anger over their socio-economic conditions – demonstrated through xenophobic violence against migrant spaza businesses – places pressure on the state and political leaders.

When residents target migrant spaza shops, their message primarily relates to the failure of the state to deliver on its economic promises. They are less concerned about the presence of shops in their neighbourhood than they are about finding ways to place the state and political leadership on edge. This is the real fear driving political attempts to curb migrant businesses; that is, uncontained anger and frustration against the political establishment. Political and state actors respond to attacks on migrant shops by clamping down on these very businesses. This placates aggrieved residents as it demonstrates that the state and ruling party are giving priority to "the people." In response to xenophobic attacks on migrant shops in 2015, the Minister of Small Business Development said that "foreigners need to understand that they are here as a courtesy and our priority is to the people of this country first and foremost."[115]

Acting against migrant spaza shops also reassures South African spaza shopkeepers and makes them less inclined to incite violence among local populations and destabilize the political status quo. In addition, focusing on the issue of migrant shopkeepers gives the impression that township economic stagnation is attributable to the presence and economic practices of foreign nationals and not the fault of government. The Inter-Ministerial Committee on Migration (IMC) thus viewed the xenophobic violence that broke out in Gauteng and KwaZulu-Natal provinces in 2015 as a consequence of economic competition from migrants and allowing too many into the country:

> *The primary cause of the violence against foreign nationals is the increased competition arising from the socio-economic circumstances in South Africa. This was illustrated by statistics showing a growth in the number of unskilled immigrants entering the country since 2008. This is in the context of slowing economic growth and a decline in unskilled job creation. This has been heightened by a decade of poor implementation of immigration and border controls.*[116]

As a result, the IMC recommended changing South Africa's migration and refugee policy, advancing township economic growth and job creation, and monitoring and licensing informal businesses.[117] It also initiated Operation Fiela ("sweep clean" in Sesotho), with the stated purpose of "eliminating criminality and general lawlessness from our communities."[118] This police and army operation largely targeted migrants and resulted in thousands being arrested or deported.[119] The then Minister in the Presidency, Jeff Radebe, said that "through Operation Fiela we are claiming our communities so that our people can live in peace."[120] These efforts give the impression that economic decline in the country is less a result of internal policy failures, and more the result of negative outside forces.

Instead of admitting their fear of discontented citizens, political leaders and other state actors display an anxiety over shops and articulate reasons to curtail them, including economic harm, illegality, business robbery rates and xenophobic crime. The problematization of migrant spaza shops is thus largely a result of unstable formal state institutions whose legitimacy is being threatened by growing popular frustration with the country's socioeconomic status quo. This leads informal political leaders and structures to incite local populations against shops (among other targets such as schools, clinics and buses) as a means of placing pressure on weak state authorities. Calls for tighter regulation of migrant spaza shops are therefore not simply a reaction to the behaviours and actions of migrant traders. They are also an outcome of the state and ruling party's tenuous authority, which leads them to use desperate populist measures to maintain control over an increasingly disillusioned populace.

CONCLUSION

Since the violent attacks in Masiphumelele in 2006, various governance actors, including police, government ministers, political parties and provincial premiers, have sought ways to curb migrant spaza shops in South Africa. These efforts have included informal trade agreements at local levels, fining migrant shops, and new legislation that prohibits asylum seekers from operating businesses in the country. A number of these interventions have overlooked the content of local by-laws and flouted legal frameworks.

Governance actors generally provide four main justifications for curbing migrant businesses in South Africa, namely, economic harm, illegality, increased business robbery rates and crime prevention. These explanations are often unsubstantiated and do not fully add up. Firstly, migrant spaza shops offer both disadvantages and advantages to local economies. While they may increase competition for South African spaza shopkeepers, they offer many economic benefits to other South Africans including landlords, consumers, suppliers and wholesalers. Secondly, fears that shops do not comply with the law do not appear to be genuine and are often exaggerated, inaccurate and do not show equal concern over potential legal violations by South African businesses. Thirdly, although reducing the number of migrant spaza shops through stricter regulation might result in a reduction in business robberies in the country, this is a problematic approach to reducing crime. One would instead expect to see strategies protecting shops and targeting perpetrators. Lastly, preventing xenophobic attacks and other violence against migrant shopkeepers through extra-legal or illegal means rather than investigating and apprehending offenders or promoting social integration, suggests that other concerns are paramount. Economic harm, illegality, business robberies and crime prevention hence do not comprehensively explain governance actions. This indicates that further considerations are at play in efforts to limit migrant spaza shops in South Africa.

In particular, efforts to curtail shops are largely driven by pressure exerted by other local actors and their ability to exploit popular discontent over enduring economic hardship in the country. Thus, political anxieties over migrant spaza shops are not primarily related to any wrongdoing on the part of migrants. Instead, the threat driving governance actions is the heightened frustration of township residents with their socio-economic conditions. When residents attack migrant spaza shops, they are expressing their dissatisfaction to an apprehensive state and political leadership. In response, these actors turn on migrant spaza shops to demonstrate their allegiance to black South African township residents, to appease South African spaza shopkeepers, and to tacitly blame socio-economic malaise on perceived foreign and external forces. Overall, governance actors do not have spaza shops primarily in mind when calling for the stricter regulation of these businesses. Instead, they are concerned about the volatile support of their key political constituencies and how this backing can be undermined or generated by the symbolic gesture of regulating the foreign spaza shop.

ENDNOTES

1   Quoted in L.. Mataboge, P. de Wet and T. Zwane, "Spazas: It's Not Just the Economy, Stupid" *Mail & Guardian*, 30 January 2015.

2   Crush (2010); Jara and Peberdy (2009); Landau (2006); Neocosmos (2006); Steinberg (2012).

3   Crush et al. (2015, 2017a, 2017b); Crush and Ramachandran (2015); Grant and Thompson (2014); Ramachandran et al. (2017).

4   Gastrow (2017).

5   Interview with Philippi East Sector Managers, Philippi East, 8 November 2011.

6   "Fleeing War, Somalis are Targets of Violence in Adopted Home" *Irin News*, 10 October 2006.

7   Government of the Western Cape (2009: 27). At: https://www.westerncape.gov.za/text/2009/3/masiphumelele_conflict_intervention_report.pdf

8   Ibid., p. 25 and 41.

9   Ibid., p. 48.

10   Ibid., p. 47.

11   Ibid., p. 32.

12   Ibid., p. 42.

13   Ibid. See also p. 43.

14   Ibid., p. 50.

15   Section 27 of the *Refugees Act* 130 of 1998 grants refugees the right to work in South Africa. Two court cases have affirmed asylum seekers' right to work in South Africa (see *Minister of Home Affairs and Others v Watchenuka and Another*, 2004 (4) SA 326 (SCA) and *Somali Association of South Africa v Limpopo Department of Economic Development, Environment and Tourism* (48/2014) ZASCA 143 (26 September 2014).

16   C. Verster, "Four Somali Shops Held Up in Past Week" *False Bay People's Post* (undated) in Gastrow (2016).

17   Ibid.

18   Interview with Somali Community Leader, Cape Town, 31 March 2015.

19   Ibid.

20   Gastrow with Amit (2010); "Toll Hits 30 After More Somalis Murdered" *IOL News*, 4 September 2006.

21   Gastrow (2016).

22   Interview with Khayelitsha Community Activist, Cape Town, 12 March 2011; Interview with Representative of the Somali Retailers Association, Bellville, 14 November 2010.

23   "General Agreement Between Zanokhanyo Retailers Association and the Somali Retailers Association in Kaylisha (sic), 27 November 2008" in Gastrow (2016).

24   "Draft Mutual Agreement Between Local and Somali Traders in Gugulethu and Other Communities in Western Cape Province, 6 August 2009" in Gastrow (2016).

25   *Competition Act* 89 of 1998, Section 4.

26   Q. Mtyala, "Somalis Refuse to Sign 'One Sided' Deal for Spaza Owners" *Cape Times*, August 2009

27   Telephone Inquiry, Competition Commission Representative, 18 March 2011.

28   Interviews with Somali traders and police in Kraaifontein, various dates.

29   SANCO Letter dated 6 May 2011 in Gastrow (2016).

30   Telephone interview with Somali Community Representative, 21 August 2012; Interview with Somali Community Representative, Bellville, 6 November 2012; Interview with Philippi East Police Officer, Philippi East, 31 October 2012; SANCO Letter to Philippi East Station Commander, 6 July 2011 in Gastrow (2016).

31   Interview with Philippi East police officer, Philippi East, 31 October 2012.

32   Interview with Somali Traders, Vredenberg, 20 February 2012.

33 E. Lewis, "We'll Close Down Illegal Spazas" *Cape Argus*, 8 February 2011.

34 L. Mkentane, "Somalis to Register with Spaza Body" *The Herald*, 25 March 2011.

35 Crush et al. (2017c).

36 Q. Mtyala. "Cele's Xenophobic Outburst" *IOL News*, 7 October 2011.

37 C. Barnes, "Cut Number of Foreign Spaza Shops – ANC" *Cape Argus,* 25 June 2012.

38 Rogerson (2015).

38 Crush et al. (2017c: 18-23).

39 DTI (2014: 10).

40 Ibid, p. 22.

41 "Laws Regulating Foreign Owned Spazas Must Be Fast Tracked: Zulu" *Morning Live on SABC News,* 27 January 2015.

42 B. Tshehle, "North West Premier Supra Mahumapelo to Bar Foreign Owned Spaza Shops" *The Sowetan*, 18 March 2016.

43 Gwede Mantashe, Secretary General of the African National Congress, Media Briefing, 20 March 2016. At: https://www.youtube.com/watch?v=mCNnWrAjIcM; "Makhura's Full Sopa Speech" *The Citizen,* 26 February 2018.

44 "Minister Rob Davies Urges Orange Farm Small Businesses to Take Advantage of Economic Opportunities Offered by Government." At: https://www.youtube.com/watch?v=BGTvJWlTSFg

45 "Draft Mutual Agreement Between Local and Somali Traders in Gugulethu and Other Communities in Western Cape Province, 6 August 2009" in Gastrow (2016).

46 Interview with Manager of Philippi Cash and Carry, Philippi East, 12 July 2012.

47 National Assembly (2015: 20).

48 Ibid.

49 Ibid., pp. 38-39.

50 "Minister Rob Davies Urges Orange Farm Small Businesses."

51 "Makhura's Full Sopa Speech."

52 Jacob Zuma at TNA Breakfast 13 February 2015. At: https://www.youtube.com/watch?v=0TRWprjhnWY

53 *Firearms Control Act* 60 of 2000, Section 9.

54 T. Petersen, "Most Illicit Cigarettes Now Made in SA – Sotyu" *News24*, 10 November 2015.

55 UNHCR Statistical Online Population Database. At: http://popstats.unhcr.org/#_ga=1.3026608.16420 08189.1414090050

56 City of Cape Town, *Informal Trading By-Law*, Provincial Gazette No. 6677, 20 November 2009. At: http://openbylaws.org.za/za/by-law/cape-town/2009/informal-trading/

57   Interview with City of Cape Town Environmental Health Officials, Bellville, 2 June 2014.

58   K. Magubane, "Reveal Trade Secrets, Minister Tells Foreigners" *Business Day*, 28 January 2015.

59   "Laws Regulating Foreign Owned Spazas Must be Fast Tracked: Zulu" *SABC News*, 27 January 2015.

60   DTI (2014: 69).

61   Speech at meeting between South African and Somali Spaza Shopkeepers, Lingelethu West Police Station, Khayelitsha, 20 March 2012.

62   Ibid.

63   Meeting between South African and Somali Spaza Shopkeepers, Lingelethu West Police Station, Khayelitsha, 20 March 2012.

64   Hikam (2011).

65   Telephone call to SARS on 15 May 2018; see also http://www.sars.gov.za/ClientSegments/Businesses/SmallBusinesses/StratingBusiness/Registering/Pages/default.aspx

66   Ibid., p. 75.

67   Gastrow and Amit (2015).

68   Mtyala, "Somalis Refuse to Sign 'One Sided' Deal."

69   *Somali Association of South Africa v Limpopo Department of Economic Development, Environment and Tourism* (48/2014) ZASCA 143 (26 September 2014), para 13.

70   Ibid.

71   The legislation cited on the fines was the *Local Authorities Act* 19 of 1974, which does not exist.

72   SAPS, *Addendum to Annual Crime Report 2015/2016*, p. 36.

73   Ibid., p. 37.

74   See crime statistics at http://www.saps.gov.za/resource_centre/publications/statistics/crimestats/2015/crime_stats.php

75   Ibid.

76   "Prologue by Lieutenant General AH Lamoer" *South African Police Service/Western Cape Annual Report 2012/2013*, p. 2.

77   Interview with South African resident, Endlovini, Khayelitsha, 6 February 2011.

78   Interview with a group of youth, Philippi East, 12 December 2011.

79   V. Cilliers, "Court Rules on Spaza Shops" *Northern News*, 24 August 2012.

80   Ibid.

81   "Agreement Between Local and Somali Traders in Gugulethu."

82   Ibid.

83   Ibid.

84 Gastrow (2016).

85 Meeting between South African and Somali Spaza Shopkeepers, Lingelethu West Police Station, Khayelitsha, 20 March 2012.

86 DTI, *National Informal Business Upliftment Strategy*.

87 Interview with Kraaifontein Police Station Detective, Kraaifontein, 13 January 2011.

88 Ibid.

89 Interview with Kraaifontein Police Station Detective, Kraaifontein, 1 December 2011.

90 Interview with Kraaifontein Somali Community Representative, Bellville, 12 December 2011; Interview with Kraaifontein Somali Community Representative, Kraaifontein, 5 June 2012.

91 Interview with Kraaifontein Police Station Detective, Kraaifontein, 1 December 2011.

92 Interviews with Khayelitsha Police Station Sector Managers and Police Colonel, Khayelitsha, 25 October 2011; Interview with Harare Police Station Detective, Harare, Khayelitsha, 7 December 2011.

93 Interview with Somali Retailers' Association Representatives, Mitchells Plain, 1 November 2010.

94 Interview with Khayelitsha Somali Community Activist, Mitchells Plain, 6 July 2012.

95 Fanon (1963); Mamdani (2001).

96 Jacob Zuma Speech to ANC members, Grand Parade, Cape Town, 9 February 2016.

97 http://www.ujuh.co.za/lindiwe-zulu-2015-small-business-dept-budget-speech/

98 Meeting between South African and Somali Spaza Shopkeepers, Lingelethu West Police Station, Khayelitsha, 20 March 2012.

99 Meeting between South African and Somali Spaza Shopkeepers at Lingelethu West Police Station, 7 March 2012.

100 Interview with South African Resident, Lower Crossroads, Philippi East, 20 January 2012.

101 Interview with South African Resident, Lower Crossroads, Philippi East, 20 January 2012.

102 Interview with South African Resident, Bloekombos, Kraaifontein, 10 August 2012.

103 Interview with South African Resident, Lower Crossroads, Philippi East, 25 January 2012.

104 Interview with South African Resident, Better Life, Philippi East, 21 January 2012.

105 Interview with South African Resident, Site C, Khayelitsha, 5 February 2011.

106 Interview with South African Resident, Gugulethu, 9 February 2011; Interview with South African Resident, Lower Crossroads, 20 January 2012.

107 R. Pather, "Xenophobic Attacks in Philippi: 'It's Like They Can't Even Think We are Human Like Them'" *The Daily Vox*, 27 February, 2015 ; D. Knoetze , "Philippi East Foreigners say Xenophobic Hatred Fuelled Attacks" *GroundUp*, 26 February 2015.

108 Interview with Khayelitsha Community Activist, Rondebosch, 28 April 2015; Interview with NGO Worker, Cape Town City Centre, 23 March 2016.

109 Interview with Philippi South African Resident, Cape Town City Centre, 22 November 2010; Interview with Khayelitsha Journalist, Rondebosch, 28 April 2015.

110 Interview with Khayelitsha Community Activist, Rondebosch, 28 April 2015.

111 Interview with Philippi South African Resident, Cape Town City Centre, 22 November 2010.

112 World Bank (2015: 2).

113 Ibid.

114 Interview with Khayelitsha Resident, Site C, Khayelitsha, 5 February 2011.

115 Magubane, "Reveal Trade Secrets, Minister Tells Foreigners. "

116 National Assembly (2015).

117 Ibid.

118 http://www.gov.za/operation-fiela

119 J. Maromo, "The Numbers Behind Operation Fiela" *Mail & Guardian*, 7 September 2015; K. Patel, "Operation Fiela and Our History of Kicking Out Illegal Immigrants" *The Daily Vox*, 28 May 2015.

120 http://reliefweb.int/report/south-africa/operation-fiela-contributing-peace-order

REFERENCES

1. Crush, J. (2010). *The Perfect Storm: The Realities of Xenophobia in Contemporary South Africa.* SAMP Migration Policy Series No. 50, Cape Town.

2. Crush, J. and Ramachadran, S. (2015). Doing Business with Xenophobia. In J. Crush, A. Chikanda and C. Skinner (Eds.), *Mean Streets: Migration, Xenophobia and Informality in South Africa.* Cape Town and Ottawa: SAMP and IDRC, pp. 25-59.

3. Crush, J., Chikanda A., and Skinner, C. (2015). Migrant Entrepreneurship and Informality in South African Cities. In J. Crush, A. Chikanda and C. Skinner (Eds.), *Mean Streets: Migration, Xenophobia and Informality in South Africa.* Cape Town and Ottawa: SAMP and IDRC, pp. 1-24.

4. Crush, J., Skinner, C., and Stulgaitis, M. (2017a). Benign Neglect or Active Destruction? A Critical Analysis of Refugee and Informal Sector Policy and Practice in South Africa. *African Human Mobility Review* 3: 751-782.

5. Crush, J., Tawodzera, G., Chikanda, A., and Tevera, D. (2017b). The Owners of Xenophobia: Zimbabwean Informal Enterprise and Xenophobic Violence in South Africa. *African Human Mobility Review* 3: 879-909.

6. Crush, J. Skinner, C. and Stulgaitis, M. (2017c). *Rendering South Africa Undesirable: A Critique of Refugee and Informal Sector Policy*, SAMP Migration Policy Series No. 79, Cape Town.

7. DTI (2014). *National Informal Business Upliftment Strategy* (Pretoria: Department of Trade and Industry).

8. Fanon, F. (1963). *The Wretched of the Earth* (New York: Grove Press).

9. Gastrow, V. (2016). Submission to the Competition Commission: Grocery Retail Enquiry. Annexures 1-8. At: http://www.compcom.co.za/wp-content/uploads/2016/09/Vanya-Gastrow-Submission.pdf

10. Gastrow, V. (2017). Shop *Gevaar*: A Socio-Legal Critique of the Governance of Foreign National Spaza Shopkeepers in South Africa. PhD Thesis, University of the Witwatersrand, Johannesburg.

11. Gastrow, V. and Amit, R. (2015). Lawless Regulation: Government and Civil Society Attempts at Regulating Somali Informal Trade in Cape Town. Report for African Centre for Migration & Society, University of the Witwatersrand, Johannesburg.

12. Gastrow, V. with Amit, R. (2010). Elusive Justice: Somali Traders Access to Formal and Informal Justice Mechanisms in the Western Cape. Report for African Centre for Migration & Society, University of the Witwatersrand, Johannesburg.

13. Government of the Western Cape (2009). Documenting and Evaluation Report: Masiphumelele Conflict Intervention: August 2006-March 2007. Cape Town.

14. Grant, R. and Thompson, D. (2014). City on Edge: Immigrant Businesses and the Right to Urban Space in Inner-City Johannesburg. *Urban Geography* 36: 181-200.

15. Hikam, A. (2011). An Exploratory Study on the Somali Immigrants' Involvement in the Informal Economy of Nelson Mandela Bay. MA dissertation, Nelson Mandela Metropolitan University.

16. Jara, M. and Peberdy, S. (2009). Progressive Humanitarian and Social Mobilisation in Neo-Apartheid Cape Town: A Report on Civil Society and the May 2008 Xenophobic Violence. Report for Atlantic Philanthropies, Johannesburg.

17. Landau, L. (2006). Transplants and Transients: Idioms of Belonging and Dislocation in Inner-City Johannesburg. (2017) *African Studies Review* 49: 125-145.

18. Mamdani, M. (2001). Beyond Settler and Native as Political Identities: Overcoming the Political Legacy of Colonialism. *Comparative Studies in Society and History* 43: 651-664.

19. National Assembly (2015). *Report by the Ad Hoc Joint Committee on Probing Violence Against Foreign Nationals.* Cape Town: South African Parliament.

20. Neocosmos, M. (2006). *From 'Foreign Natives' to 'Native Foreigners': Explaining Xeno-phobia in Post Apartheid South Africa: Citizenship and Nationalism, Identity and Politics* (Dakar: Codesria).

21. Ramachandran, S., Crush, J. and Tawodzera, G. (2017). Security Risk and Xenophobia in the Urban Informal Sector. *African Human Mobility Review* 3: 854-878.

22. Rogerson, C. (2015). Unpacking National Policy Towards the Urban Informal Economy. In J. Crush, A. Chikanda and C. Skinner (Eds.), *Mean Streets: Migration, Xenophobia and Informality in South Africa.* Cape Town and Ottawa: SAMP and IDRC, pp. 229-248

23. Steinberg, J. (2012). Security and Disappointment: Policing, Freedom and Xenophobia in South Africa. *British Journal of Criminology* 52: 345-360.

24. World Bank (2015). *South Africa Economic Update: 2015* (Washington DC: World Bank).

MIGRATION POLICY SERIES

1 *Covert Operations: Clandestine Migration, Temporary Work and Immigration Policy in South Africa* (1997) ISBN 1-874864-51-9

2 *Riding the Tiger: Lesotho Miners and Permanent Residence in South Africa* (1997) ISBN 1-874864-52-7

3 *International Migration, Immigrant Entrepreneurs and South Africa's Small Enterprise Economy* (1997) ISBN 1-874864-62-4

4 *Silenced by Nation Building: African Immigrants and Language Policy in the New South Africa* (1998) ISBN 1-874864-64-0

5 *Left Out in the Cold? Housing and Immigration in the New South Africa* (1998) ISBN 1-874864-68-3

6 *Trading Places: Cross-Border Traders and the South African Informal Sector* (1998) ISBN 1-874864-71-3

7 *Challenging Xenophobia: Myth and Realities about Cross-Border Migration in Southern Africa* (1998) ISBN 1-874864-70-5

8 *Sons of Mozambique: Mozambican Miners and Post-Apartheid South Africa* (1998) ISBN 1-874864-78-0

31 *Migration, Sexuality and HIV/AIDS in Rural South Africa* (2004) ISBN 1-919798-63-3

32 *Swaziland Moves: Perceptions and Patterns of Modern Migration* (2004) ISBN 1-919798-67-6

33 *HIV/AIDS and Children's Migration in Southern Africa* (2004) ISBN 1-919798-70-6

34 *Medical Leave: The Exodus of Health Professionals from Zimbabwe* (2005) ISBN 1-919798-74-9

35 *Degrees of Uncertainty: Students and the Brain Drain in Southern Africa* (2005) ISBN 1-919798-84-6

36 *Restless Minds: South African Students and the Brain Drain* (2005) ISBN 1-919798-82-X

37 *Understanding Press Coverage of Cross-Border Migration in Southern Africa since 2000* (2005) ISBN 1-919798-91-9

38 *Northern Gateway: Cross-Border Migration Between Namibia and Angola* (2005) ISBN 1-919798-92-7

39 *Early Departures: The Emigration Potential of Zimbabwean Students* (2005) ISBN 1-919798-99-4

40 *Migration and Domestic Workers: Worlds of Work, Health and Mobility in Johannesburg* (2005) ISBN 1-920118-02-0

41 *The Quality of Migration Services Delivery in South Africa* (2005) ISBN 1-920118-03-9

42 *States of Vulnerability: The Future Brain Drain of Talent to South Africa* (2006) ISBN 1-920118-07-1

43 *Migration and Development in Mozambique: Poverty, Inequality and Survival* (2006) ISBN 1-920118-10-1

44 *Migration, Remittances and Development in Southern Africa* (2006) ISBN 1-920118-15-2

45 *Medical Recruiting: The Case of South African Health Care Professionals* (2007) ISBN 1-920118-47-0

46 *Voices From the Margins: Migrant Women's Experiences in Southern Africa* (2007) ISBN 1-920118-50-0

47 *The Haemorrhage of Health Professionals From South Africa: Medical Opinions* (2007) ISBN 978-1-920118-63-1

48 *The Quality of Immigration and Citizenship Services in Namibia* (2008) ISBN 978-1-920118-67-9

49 *Gender, Migration and Remittances in Southern Africa* (2008) ISBN 978-1-920118-70-9

50 *The Perfect Storm: The Realities of Xenophobia in Contemporary South Africa* (2008) ISBN 978-1-920118-71-6

51 *Migrant Remittances and Household Survival in Zimbabwe* (2009) ISBN 978-1-920118-92-1

52 *Migration, Remittances and 'Development' in Lesotho* (2010) ISBN 978-1-920409-26-5

53 *Migration-Induced HIV and AIDS in Rural Mozambique and Swaziland* (2011) ISBN 978-1-920409-49-4

54 *Medical Xenophobia: Zimbabwean Access to Health Services in South Africa* (2011) ISBN 978-1-920409-63-0

55 *The Engagement of the Zimbabwean Medical Diaspora* (2011) ISBN 978-1-920409-64-7

56 *Right to the Classroom: Educational Barriers for Zimbabweans in South Africa* (2011) ISBN 978-1-920409-68-5